Bears, Bears, and More Bears

Jackie Morris

BARRON'S

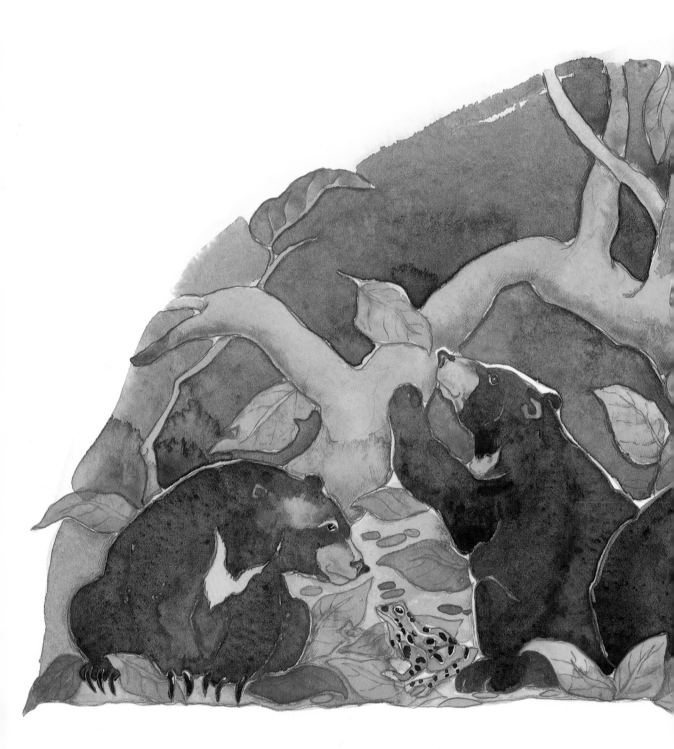

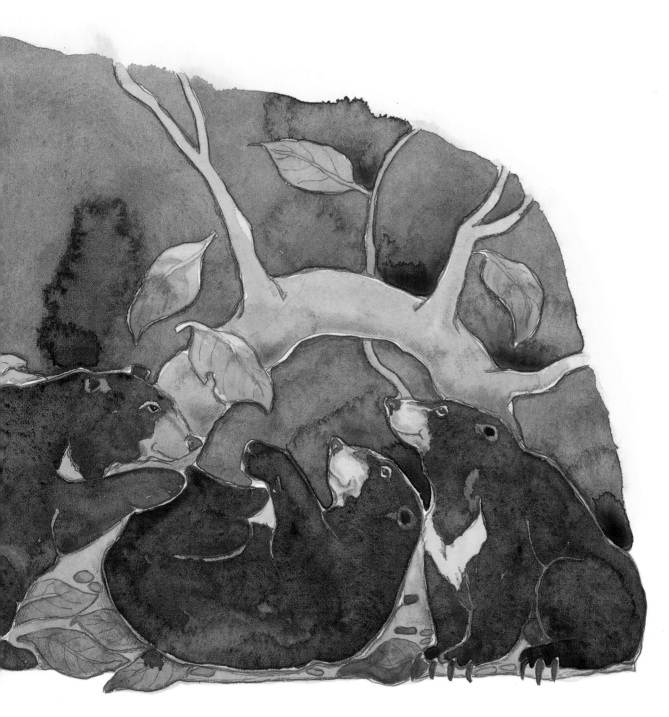

There are little bears.

There are big bears.

Bears can be black.

Bears can be brown.

Bears can even be white.

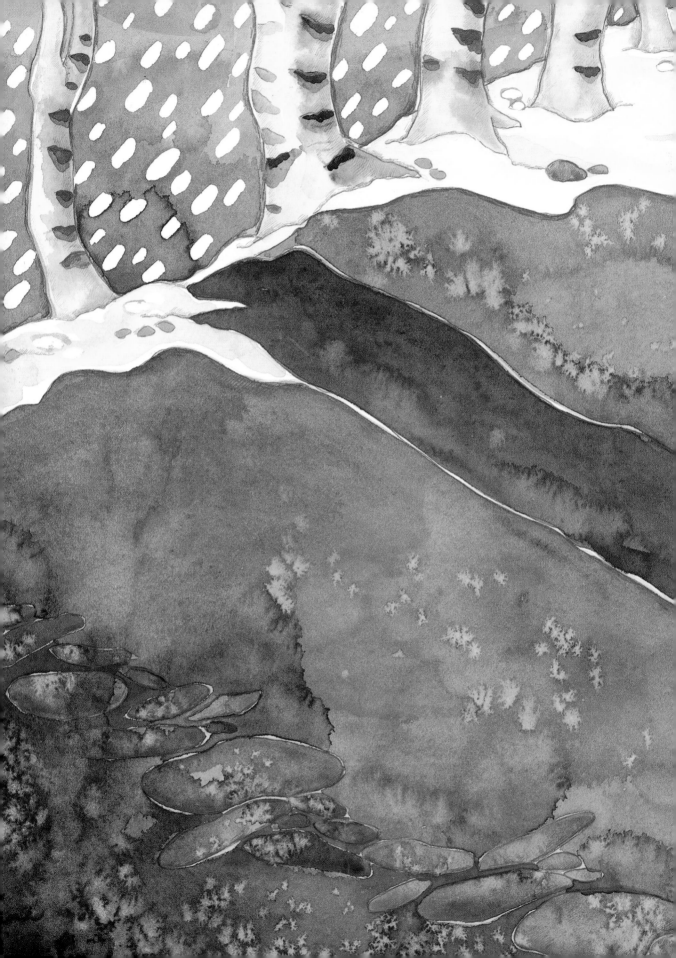

Most bears sleep all winter.

Most bears climb trees...

...run very fast

and swim.

Some bears eat berries;

some eat fish.

Some bears eat bamboo.

Some bears aren't

real bears at all.

are lots of bears in the world.

But the best bear is your bear.

There are little bears.

- *Sun Bears are the smallest bears.*
- *They weigh between 60 and 145 pounds (27 and 65 kg) and are 4 to 5 feet (1.2 to 1.5 meters) high/long.*
- *Sun Bears are very rare.*
- *They live in the forests of Southeast Asia, where they are often kept as pets.*

There are big bears.

- *American Brown Bears, also called Grizzly Bears, are very big.*
- *They can weigh as much as 800 pounds (390 kg).*
- *However, the largest bear of all is the Polar Bear. It can weigh up to 1,320 pounds (600 kg) and is 8 to 9 feet (2.4 to 2.6 meters) high/long.*

Bears can be black.

- *The Asiatic Black Bear lives in the forests and mountains of Asia.*
- *These bears have a golden crest on their chest and a mane of long black hair.*
- *There is also an American Black Bear, which is a large black bear with a brown muzzle.*

Bears can be brown.

- *The Brown Bear is the most common bear.*
- *Brown Bears live in Northern Canada and all over Russia.*
- *They have a distinct hump on their shoulders and very long claws on their front paws.*

Bears can even be white.

- *Polar Bears live in the Arctic where their white color camouflages them against the snow.*
- *Their diet consists of fish, seal, and the occasional walrus.*

Most bears sleep all winter.

- *Most bears sleep for about five to seven months in a year.*
- *Bears sleep in dens where the cubs are born in late winter.*
- *The dens help to keep the cubs safe when young.*
- *Bears usually have between one and four cubs, though two is the most common.*

Most bears climb trees . . .

- *Even the Grizzly Bear can climb trees.*
- *Bears climb mainly for safety, but they also climb to look for food, or simply to sun themselves and rest.*

. . . run very fast, and swim.

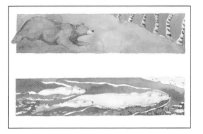

- *Bears can only run in short bursts, but they can reach high speeds.*
- *Polar Bears can run as fast as 25 miles (40 km) per hour.*
- *Most bears can swim, but Polar Bears swim underwater to catch their food.*

Some bears eat berries; some eat fish.

- *Berries and roots make up 60 to 90 percent of most bears' diets.*
- *Polar Bears usually eat fish, but even they eat grass in the summer.*
- *All bears love honey.*

Some bears eat bamboo.

- *Bamboo makes up almost all of a Giant Panda's diet.*
- *Adults eat about 27 pounds (12.5 kg) a day, sometimes eating for up to 17 hours. The rest of the time they sleep.*

Some bears aren't real bears at all.

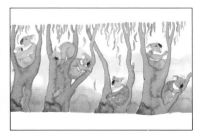

- *Koala Bears are actually marsupials, which means they carry their young in a pouch.*
- *They live in Australia and eat Eucalyptus leaves.*

First edition for the United States published in 1995 by Barron's Educational Series, Inc.

First published in 1995 by Piccadilly Press Ltd
5 Castle Road, London, NW1 8PR United Kingdom

Text and illustrations copyright © Jackie Morris, 1995

All inquiries should be addressed to:
Barron's Educational Series, Inc.
250 Wireless Boulevard
Hauppauge, New York 11788

International Standard Book No. 0-8120-6516-6 (hardcover)
0-8120-9349-6 (paperback)
Library of Congress Catalog Card No. 94-42980

Library of Congress Cataloging-in-Publication Data
Morris, Jackie.
[Just bears]
Bears, bears, and more bears / Jackie Morris.
p.   cm.
Previously published as: Just bears.
ISBN 0-8120-6516-6 (hc). — ISBN 0-8120-9349-6 (pbk.)
1. Bears—Juvenile literature. [1. Bears.] I. Title.
QL737.C27M675   1995
599.74'446—dc20
94-42980
CIP
AC

Printed in Hong Kong
5678   987654321